Samuel Barber

A Hand of Bridge

For four solo voices
and chamber orchestra

text
by
Gian
Carlo
Menotti

Ed. 2354

G. SCHIRMER, Inc.

DISTRIBUTED BY
HAL•LEONARD®
CORPORATION
7777 W. BLUEMOUND RD. P.O. BOX 13819 MILWAUKEE, WI 53213

NOTE

CHARACTERS

DAVID, a florid businessman . . . . Baritone

GERALDINE, his middle-aged wife . . . . Soprano

BILL, a lawyer . . . . Tenor

SALLY, his wife . . . . Contralto

Duration: Approximately 9 minutes.

First performed at the Festival of Two Worlds in Spoleto, Italy, June 17, 1959.

Note for Staging

The performance in order to be effective must not deny the static quality of the libretto but, if anything, should intensify it. The histrionic element should be supplied by lighting changes and by the expression of the singers who should not be allowed to leave the card table under any circumstances. While each character sings his interior monologue, enclosed (   ) in the score, the other three should remain more or less in darkness and remain frozen in an attitude. This staging device, of course, can also be reversed; that is to say that the character singing the monologue may be immobile while the others continue playing bridge.

G. C. M.; S. B.

A Hand Of Bridge

Text by Gian Carlo Menotti

Music by Samuel Barber, Op. 35
Piano reduction by the composer

One heart.

Two clubs.

sempre stacc.

44590C

Two hearts.

Five clubs.

Four hearts.

Pass.

sempre stacc.

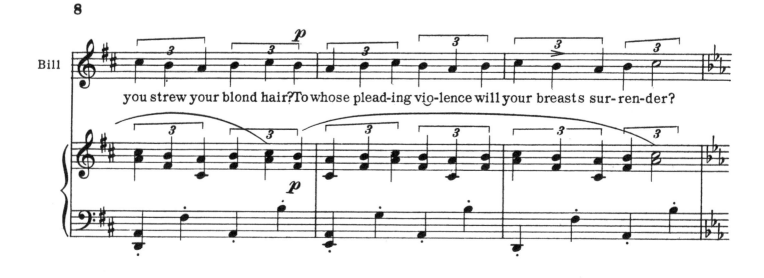

Bill: you strew your blond hair? To whose plead-ing vio-lence will your breasts sur-ren-der?

Sally: (I want to buy that hat of pea-cock feath-ers!)

Bill: Is it Chris-to-pher, Ol-i-ver, Mor-ti-mer, Man-fred, Chuck,

Bill: Tom-my or Dom-i-nic? Cym-ba-line, Cym-ba-line! Oh, if on-ly you

(What is he think-ing of _____ that he plays so dis-tract-ed-ly?

Sure-ly not of his wife,— the long dis-card-ed

Queen; Sure-ly not of me _____ whose

Sostenuto, un poco mosso ♩= 54

foot he no long-er seeks un-der the card ta-ble.

Who is there to

love me? Who is there for me to love?

But there she lies___ in her pain, co - cooned in her

ill - ness,___ an in-dif-f'rent stran-ger, hatch-ing for her-

self___ the black wings of death.___

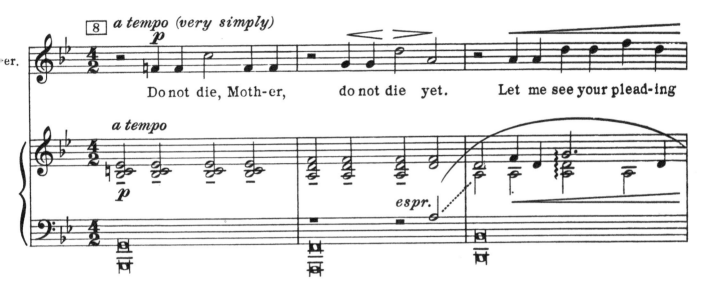

8 *a tempo (very simply)*

Do not die, Moth-er, do not die yet. Let me see your plead-ing

eyes once more_____ Now that, at last,___ I am learn-ing to

poco allarg.

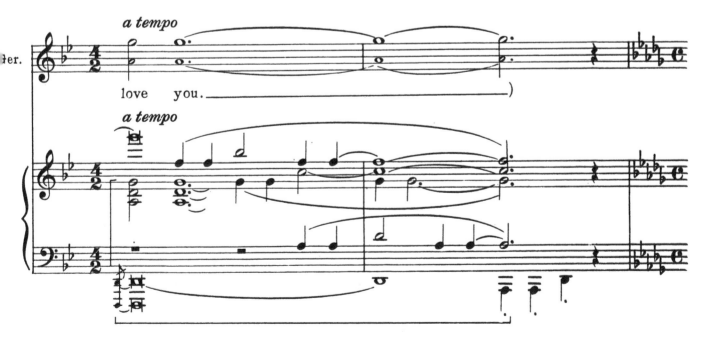

love you._____)

a tempo

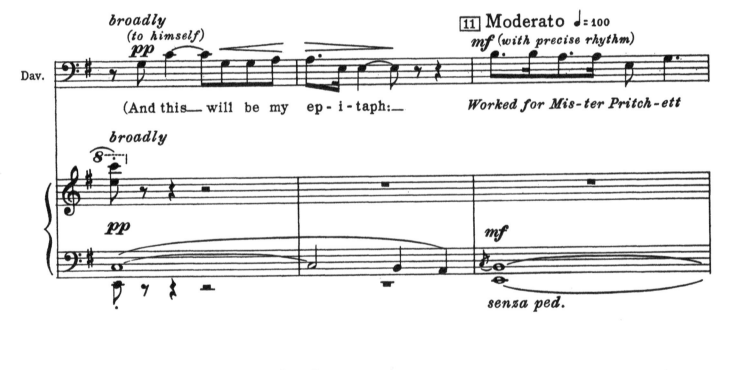

19

44590

Dav.

I could be a king, the King of Dia - monds, ___ the

p

senza ped.

pochiss. rall.

mf

mp

Dav.

Sul - tan of A - mer - i - ca! An

pochiss. rall.

mf

mp

13 *a tempo*

Dav.

al - a - bas - ter pal - ace in ___ Palm ___ Beach,

a tempo

legato

poco f,
sonoro

I keep hid-den_____ in the li-brar-y be-hind the *Who's Who*.___ To

whip a love - ly Nu - bian slave____ for____ fun:

or, bet-ter still,___ Mis-ter Pritchett,___ the bas-tard!

still play bridge each eve-ning with Sal - ly and Bill. —

Or Mis-ter Pritch-ett! — Oh, nev - er, nev- er would I own —

twen - ty na - ked boys — or twen- ty na - ked girls... —

44590

Ger. (Do not die, Moth-er, do not die_____

now.)_____

Sally Hearts.

Bill Hearts.

Dav. Trump!

meno mosso

a tempo, con moto

senza ped.

sempre stacc.

senza ped.